# How to Do Homework Without Throwing Up

by Trevor Romain

Illustrated by Steve Mark

free spirit
PUBLISHING®

**Library of Congress Cataloging-in-Publication Data**
Names: Romain, Trevor, author. | Mark, Steve, illustrator.
Title: How to do homework without throwing up / Trevor Romain ; illustrated by Steve Mark.
Description: Revised and updated edition. | Minneapolis : Free Spirit Publishing, 2017. |
    Series: Laugh & learn | Includes index.
Identifiers: LCCN 2016037937 | ISBN 9781631980664 (paperback) | ISBN 1631980661
    (paperback) | ISBN 9781631981494 (ePub) | ISBN 9781631981487 (Web PDF)
Subjects: LCSH: Homework—Juvenile literature. | BISAC: JUVENILE NONFICTION / Social
    Issues / Self-Esteem & Self-Reliance. | JUVENILE NONFICTION / Study Aids / General.
Classification: LCC LB1048 .R59 2017 | DDC 371.30281—dc23 LC record available at
    https://lccn.loc.gov/2016037937

Reading Level Grade 4; Interest Level Ages 8–13;
Fountas & Pinnell Guided Reading Level S

Edited by Elizabeth Verdick and Eric Braun
Designed by Emily Dyer

10 9 8 7 6 5 4 3 2 1
Printed in the United States of America
V20300217

**Free Spirit Publishing Inc.**
6325 Sandburg Road, Suite 100
Minneapolis, MN 55427-3674
(612) 338-2068
help4kids@freespirit.com
www.freespirit.com

# Dedication

To my second-grade teacher, Mrs. Varrie,
who taught me how to make friends
with my homework.

# Contents

# Chapter 1
# Do Not Read This!

You peeked! Ha! Now that I have your attention, I must tell you that this book is about homework. That's right . . .

Before you say, "Homework, who needs it?" think again. You need it, my friend. It's not just there to make your life miserable.

Here are a few good reasons for doing homework:

- It helps you practice skills that you haven't fully learned yet. And it helps you review skills that you have learned.

- It gives you the chance to finish up tasks that you couldn't get done during school hours.

- It helps you learn and grow.

# Why Me? You Ask

Everybody who goes to school does homework. You are not alone. And other kids feel just as sick as you do when they have to do homework.

Kids have been doing homework for hundreds of years. And for hundreds of years homework has been driving children from around the world crazy.

Homework was not invented to spoil your day or get in the way of your fun, although sometimes it feels that way. I know, because I had to do homework while writing this book to find some of the information I have included in it. My homework got in the way of some of the things I would have rather been doing, and it took some planning and organization to get it all done. Many of the tips and tricks I used to get my homework done are in this book.

Hanging out instead of going home and doing your homework is called **procrastinating.** Procrastinating means: I'll think of a thousand things to do to keep me from doing my homework.

Do not pull out your hair because you have homework to do. (The homework won't get done, and you'll go bald.)

People who say homework is a waste of time don't know what they're talking about. They'll probably grow up without useful skills and might end up with jobs they really don't like.

A lot of people don't realize this, but homework actually makes you smarter. Now maybe you're thinking, "Say what? Nuh-uh. That's impossible." But it's true. Focusing on your homework and doing the best job you can will help you understand the work better and improve your grades.

It sounds so simple. And it is. Even very, very smart people have to do homework. And, believe it or not, some people who once had poor grades have become very smart by concentrating on their homework and learning from it.

# The Great Homework Battle

Throwing a fit will not make your homework easier to do. It will probably just get you grounded!

You cannot make your homework disappear! It will not vanish into thin air. If you try to get rid of your homework, it will just come back the next day to haunt you.

You cannot escape homework. It will follow you wherever you go. Even to the North Pole. Get to your homework before it gets to you.

Do not fight or argue with your homework! You will lose. The best way to get your homework done without feeling sick every time you see it is to just do it.

In fact, if you have any homework at the moment, put down this book and go do it. You'll feel great afterward, and you'll be able to enjoy what you're reading without having that nagging "uh-oh, gotta do my homework" feeling in the back of your mind.

Do not blame the contents of your room for your homework. Breaking your pencil into a thousand pieces, kicking your desk, attacking the lamp, or yelling at your teddy bear will **NOT** make your homework do itself. **YOU** must do it.

Even though you pray as hard as you can pray, wish as hard as you can wish, cry as hard as you can cry, HOMEWORK HAPPENS!

# 10 Terrible Excuses for Not Doing Your Homework

I hate to be the one to tell you this, but excuses will only create stress and trouble. Instead of thinking up really good excuses, use that time to just do your homework.

1. I DON'T FEEL LIKE iT.

2. NO TIME.

3. HOMEWORK? WHAT HOMEWORK?

4. I LEFT iT AT SCHOOL, ON THE BUS, iN THE CAFETERIA . . .

5. I HAVE TO WATCH MY FAVORITE TV SHOW.

6. NOBODY REMINDED ME.

7. HOMEWORK iS REALLY, REALLY, REALLY, REALLY BOR-iNG.

8. I HAVE BETTER THiNGS TO DO.

9. I DIDN'T WRiTE DOWN THE ASSIGNMENT.

10. MY DOG MIGHT EAT iT.

## Chapter 2

# 7 Tips for Getting Started

## TIP #1 Get It Done BEFORE You Get Home

Here's a GREAT thing about homework. You get to do it at home!

But that doesn't mean you have to wait until you get home. Although the word "home" is in homework, you can do your homework on the bus, especially if it's something like reading. You can do homework at an after-school program if you go to one. You can even do homework while waiting for sports practice or singing lessons. In fact, anytime you find yourself waiting, instead of sighing, rolling your eyes, and counting the minutes, do a little homework.

Use any spare time—like study periods at school—to do your homework. Most schools have a place where you can work quietly, like in a study room or at the library. Just ask your teacher for a suggestion. The more homework you can do during spare time at school, the more time you'll have to play hard and have fun when you're at home.

# TIP #2 Make a Homework Schedule

This will tell you exactly when to do your homework and when to do all the really fun stuff that keeps you from doing homework.

Hang your schedule on the fridge or in your room so you don't forget about it. (BONUS TIP: Do not crumple up, mangle, spit on, sneeze on, throw up on, wipe your dirty fingers on, or tear into a million pieces your homework schedule!)

You can also enter your schedule into a calendar on your phone, tablet, or computer. Set your device to remind you when to get started.

## The D (for Duh) Homework Schedule

4:00 to 7:30 Play outdoors, feed the dog, eat dinner, play video games, watch YouTube videos, feed goldfish, read comic book, pick nose, twiddle thumbs, stare at the ceiling for the longest time.

7:30 to 9:30 Do it all again and binge-watch your favorite new TV series.

9:30 Go to bed.

9:31 Stare at the ceiling again, remember the big major homework assignment you didn't do, sweat profusely, bite fingernails, wish for a giant snowstorm to happen so you won't have to go to school tomorrow.

### The A+ Homework Schedule

4:00 to 4:30 Play outdoors, have a quick and
  healthy snack.

4:30 to 5:30 Homework time! Breathe deeply, do
  homework, think hard, stretch, think harder.

5:30 to 7:00 Stop homework, play, feed the dog,
  call a friend, eat dinner.

7:00 to 8:00 Finish up any remaining homework.

8:00 to 9:30 Free time (if your homework is done).

9:30 Go to bed, sleep like a baby, dream about
  how happy your teacher will be about your
  completed homework!

# TIP #3 Find a Homework Helper

Get a good friend, parent, or relative to help you with your homework. A homework helper will help you understand things.

Some kids don't want to do their homework because they don't want to miss out on playing with friends. Let's be honest: Playing can sometimes, occasionally, *maybe* be more fun than homework. To solve that problem, some kids look for homework buddies. You can try to find friends who live near you and start a homework club where you all do your homework together.

# TIP #4 Have a Healthy Snack

Try to eat something before you do your homework. It's easier to concentrate if you are not thinking about food.

**FOOD FOR THOUGHT:** Your brain needs fuel to run on. Foods high in proteins, carbohydrates, and vitamins can provide that fuel. Foods high in fat weigh you down. Fats are hard to digest, so they keep blood in the stomach area and not in the brain (where you want it!).

Feed your brain healthy snacks and drink a glass of water or milk. Caffeinated drinks like soda and energy drinks will energize you for a little while, but then you'll just feel more tired later.

**NOTE:** Don't snack on your pencil. Chewing on your pencil while doing your homework is not good for your gums. Plus, you get gross flecks of yellow stuff stuck between your teeth.

## Great **Pre-Homework Snacks (for energy):**

- Peanut butter and jelly sandwich

- Carrots and celery

- Granola bar

- Fruit

- Popcorn

- Yogurt

## Not-So-Great Pre-Homework Snacks:

- Two candy bars
- A handful of chocolate chip cookies
- A double bacon cheeseburger and fries
- Leftover candy from last Halloween
- Super-Duper-Sugar brand cereal
- An entire bag of potato chips
- A high-caffeine soft drink

FULL O' FAT CHIPS

# TIP #5 Clear Your Head

Before you do your homework, spend a few seconds breathing deeply. Push interfering thoughts out of your mind.

## "Ping. Ping. Ping."

Uh-oh. The sound of a phone or tablet announcing texts or alerts is very distracting for people doing homework. If you have a phone, turn it off or leave it in another room. It will help you keep a clear mind, make your homework less stressful to do, and make it easier, too. (And your cat's catnap won't be interrupted.)

# TIP #6 Prioritize

Pick the hardest homework to do first. Save the easiest for last. This means the more you do your homework, the easier it gets.

# TIP #7 Go to Your Homework Zone

Do your homework in the same place every day. This way, the minute you sit down, you automatically switch into homework mode. As time goes by, this will become a routine and doing your homework will become easier.

During homework time, leave your digital media devices in another room. If you keep your electronics close by, you will be tempted to use them instead of doing your homework. They will keep calling you. "Pssst. Forget about that homework. Come play with me, I'm a lonely video game. I'll teach you how to get to level 3. Homework is for other people, not you."

# Chapter 3

# 9 Hints for Doing (And Get-Throughing) your Homework

## HINT #1 Go Screen-Free

You cannot watch television or videos—or play games on your phone, or text, or get on social media—and do your homework at the same time. It doesn't work! People who do their homework while looking at screens often develop "Screen-Homework-Neck." (This is a nervous twitch of the head that occurs as a result of continually flicking your head up, down, or over to get a quick look at the screen as you work.) The more you flick, the more you twitch. The more you twitch, the more you flick.

This terrible condition gets worse as you age. "Screen-Homework-Neck" is embarrassing when you get old enough to kiss and you keep missing the other person's mouth.

Many kids do their homework on a computer, tablet, or other electronic device. These devices make it very tempting to be distracted. It's so easy to switch over to another app to play or watch videos! To stay focused, you have to be strong! Make a deal with yourself that you will do `homework only` for 30 minutes, then reward yourself with five minutes of playtime. Some kids turn off Wi-Fi on their devices until they have completed their homework.

# HINT #2 Slow Down

Homework has a **SPEED LIMIT!** Do not write or type faster than 65 miles per hour. If you do your homework at excessive speeds, you'll miss turns, hit bumps, and lose your way. (And your homework might burst into flames.)

# HINT #3 Increase the Peace

If noise bothers you while you do your homework, tell everyone in your home to PLEASE BE QUIET! If they don't listen, call a family meeting and say, "Hey, I am a responsible student. I am dedicated to furthering my education. I am determined to be successful. So . . . please HUSH, for goodness sake!"

If you can't control the noise, find somewhere else to do your work. Maybe you can stay at the school library after school or go outside.

# HINT #4 Give Yourself a Break

Sometimes it helps to have a little intermission while you're doing your homework. Little breaks during homework help refresh your mind.

When I say little break, I mean a LITTLE break of five minutes. Not a four-hour break that includes three videos, a basketball game, two pieces of toast, teasing the neighbor's dog, reading all your comic books, and playing video games.

The best breaks are ones that let you move. Get away from the desk or screen you have been working on. Do something physical, like taking a quick walk or petting your dog.

# HINT #5 Don't Be Gross

Avoid picking your nose or pulling out your eyebrow hairs while doing homework. This will only distract you.

# HINT #6 Remember: Homework Can Be Useful!

If you want something from your mom or dad, the best way to get it is to use your completed homework as a tool. To make this work really well for you, use the words, "I've done my homework," after every sentence. For effective results, always drop your voice when you say "done my homework." For example: "Mom, can I meet my friends to see the new superhero movie? I've done my homework. It's playing at the theater in the mall. I've done my homework. And could you drive me there because I have . . . done my homework."

Doing your homework makes parents very happy. A happy parent will make you happy, and a happy you will make your homework easier to do.

# HINT #7 Read!

Reading makes homework a lot easier to do. The more you read, the better you'll understand things. It's quite amazing. Without even knowing it, you'll get smarter. Reading opens your mind like a key opens a lock. It's automatic!

For practice, read anything and everything: great literature, poems, novels, blogs, websites, nonfiction, plays, short stories, mysteries, magazines, newspapers, journals, your big sister's diary (OOPS! Just kidding!), maps, comic books, road signs, billboards, cereal boxes—the list goes on and on!

# HINT #8 Get Help for Extra Challenges

Sometimes kids have a problem with homework because they simply can't see what's on the board. If you have trouble seeing what the teacher is writing, you might need glasses. (When I was young, I had a problem with homework until my mother took me to the eye doctor. My whole life changed when I started wearing glasses. I could see!)

Sometimes people with learning differences like ADHD or dyslexia find it difficult to focus on homework. Some kids might have other distractions like being bullied or problems at home. If something is distracting you and makes your homework difficult, please ask an adult for help.

# HINT #9 Be an Active Learner at School

Participating in class makes homework easier to do because the more involved you get, the better you'll understand what you're being taught.

# Chapter 4

# A Few Things That WON'T Help with Homework (And What WILL Help Instead)

In class, it is **NOT** a good idea to copy or cheat. Instead, think for yourself. If you keep asking other people for the answers, you won't understand the material and your homework will be hard to complete.

If you sleep in class, you won't even know that you have homework to do!

### Feeling down . . .

**. . . or depressed** about your homework means you need help. Ask your teacher or parent for help. They might suggest that you get a tutor. A tutor can teach you things you're having trouble understanding and will help you sharpen your skills. Don't be afraid to get a tutor.

Some kids feel really upset, sad, or cranky a lot of the time. Kids who often feel really down or blue might need to get help from a counselor or therapist. Talk to an adult like a parent or teacher about getting help.

Once you've received the help you need, you'll feel **A LOT** better about your homework and about yourself.

Drinking alcohol or using drugs does NOT make homework easier to do. It just makes you a dope!

If your school provides laptops, tablets, or other devices to students to use for doing schoolwork, you most likely have rules you have to follow. You're probably not supposed to play games on your device, and you know you should not look at inappropriate websites.

Follow the rules and don't use your tablet as a plate for your pizza or to balance a short table leg. Take care of the equipment the school has trusted you with. That way the school can keep giving kids these cool tools!

You shouldn't fear your homework. Your homework should fear **YOU!** (Simply because you can take care of your homework anytime you want to.)

Your teacher didn't invent homework, so don't try to make your teacher's life miserable. For example, do **NOT** stick a big piece of gooey chewed-up bubblegum on your teacher's chair!

You cannot bribe your teacher with an apple or even a homemade apple pie. (Bribing means giving your teacher a gift so that he or she will not give you homework.) Don't even try it!

If the sight of your homework makes you want to puke, do NOT suffer in silence. Instead, let your teacher know. Say, "Sir (or Ma'am), I'm going to throw up all over this homework because I don't understand it. I feel green, I have a headache, and I'm afraid I'm going to fail. I need some help, please."

Believe it or not, most teachers will not yell at you or make you feel stupid. Your teacher will HELP you. That's why your teacher is there.

NO! Your teacher will not believe the toilet ate your homework. And your teacher will not believe the dog ate your homework either. DOGS DO NOT EAT HOMEWORK! A dog will throw up if it tries to eat any type of homework, especially if it's a science project.

Definitely do not get into the bad habit of skipping your homework. Turn your homework into a good habit, like brushing your teeth. Soon you won't even know you're doing it.

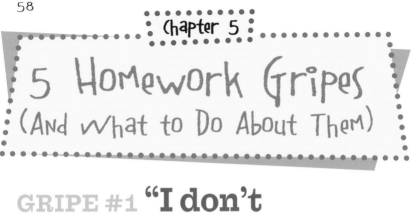

**Chapter 5**

# 5 Homework Gripes (And What to Do About Them)

## GRIPE #1 "I don't have time."

Make time. Remember this: Homework is not optional!

The whole reason you have to do homework is to help you understand what you are learning at school. It's like a skateboard. The front wheels are school, and the back wheels are homework. As you know, it would be difficult to skate smoothly with only the front wheels while the back drags on the ground.

TICK TOCK

# GRIPE #2 "I don't understand it."

Ask your teacher for help before the school day is over. Do all the parts you can do, then figure out where you're stuck. At home, do not be afraid to ask an adult or your older brother or sister to help you.

Lots of times you can find help online. Your school or school district might have a homework help website. Khan Academy is a free online resource where you can learn more about math, science, and many other subjects. Material is taught with videos by experts. Check it out at www.khanacademy.org. Or try Crash Course Kids. This YouTube channel has tons of short, entertaining videos that teach all sorts of elementary school topics. (Tell your teacher that the videos are aligned with curriculum standards, and maybe she'll let you watch them in class!) Visit www.youtube.com/user/crashcoursekids.

# GRIPE #3 "I can't ever finish it."

Find out why. Are you distracted? Are you having trouble in a certain subject? Ask your teacher or a parent for some advice about managing your time.

# GRIPE #4 "I have too much homework."

Organize yourself. Make a homework schedule that says what you'll do and when you'll do it. Use a calendar to remind yourself of short-term and long-term assignments. Do not procrastinate! Ask your teacher to give you advance notice of upcoming projects so you can get an early start.

# GRIPE #5 "I forget to bring my books home."

Remind yourself each day before you leave school to do a `Backpack Check.` Do you have everything you need? Write little reminders to yourself on your notebooks, posted in your locker, on your phone, on your hand—whatever works for you.

Make sure you know exactly what homework is expected and when you need to turn it in. One sure way to make parents or caregivers really grumpy and mad is to forget all about your homework so they have to phone your best friend's parent late at night to find out what the homework assignments were. Don't let this happen to you.

# Chapter 6

# That Awesome Feeling When You Finish Homework

A great thing about finishing your homework is that you'll have free time to spend with your friends and family—without that nagging "uh-oh, gotta do my homework" feeling. After you've worked so hard, you'll have a great time watching a movie, playing lacrosse, posting ridiculous photos online, going out for dinner, or spending the rest of the day doing things you love to do.

**WARNING!** Homework has serious side effects. You might become smart and successful if you do all your homework!

You'll not only feel relieved when you complete your homework, but you'll also feel proud. Being proud of what you do boosts your self-esteem. So, doing a good job on your homework can actually make you feel great about your accomplishments and yourself all at the same time.

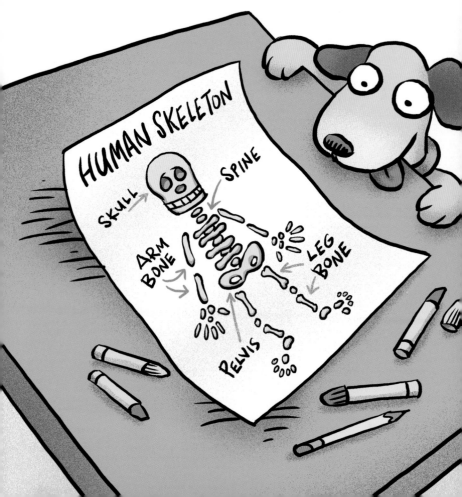

# 7 Quick Reminders

- Do your homework in the same place every time. Make sure it's a quiet place with the TV and other devices turned off.

- Eat a meal or light snack before doing your homework.

- Do the hardest assignment first.

- Ask your teacher for help when you need it. (TIP: Do this while you're still at school. Desperately telephoning your teacher at midnight is NOT a good idea.)

- Find a homework helper if you need one. This can be a good friend, a classmate, a sibling, or a parent. (Your goldfish cannot be a homework helper.)

- Ask your family to respect your homework time. If you want, put a "Do Not Disturb" sign on your door (or on your forehead).

- Take little breaks during your homework time. Stand up and stretch, get a drink of water or an energizing snack, or do 10 jumping jacks—whatever keeps you going.

# The Nicest Thing

The nicest thing about doing your homework is the feeling you get when it's DONE!

Nothing is better than this feeling. That homework is gone. Finished. Outta here! It's like waking up from a stressful dream. If you just hate doing homework, try to think of how great you are going to feel when it is done.

Doing your homework to the best of your ability will one day help you reach as high as you can reach and go as far as you want to go!

# Index

# About the Author and Illustrator

When **Trevor Romain** was 12, his teacher told him he wasn't talented enough to do art. By accident, he found out 20 years later that he could draw. Since that lucky day, he has written and illustrated more than 50 books for children. His books have sold more than a million copies worldwide and have been published in 18 different languages. Trevor also travels to schools, hospitals, summer camps, and military bases throughout the world, delivering stand-up comedy with inspirational self-help messages to hundreds of thousands of school-age children.

Trevor, who is passionate about helping young people face and overcome tough challenges, has been the president of the American Childhood Cancer Organization and is well known for his work with the Make-A-Wish Foundation, the United Nations, UNICEF, USO, and the Comfort Crew for Military Kids, which he co-founded. He has performed on multiple USO tours, has visited and worked with former child soldiers and at refugee camps and orphanages, and has worked with the United Nations developing educational materials for children living in armed conflict areas.

**Steve Mark** is a freelance illustrator and a part-time puppeteer. He lives in Minnesota and is the father of three and the husband of one. Steve has illustrated several books in the Laugh & Learn series, including *Don't Behave Like You Live in a Cave* and *Bullying Is a Pain in the Brain*.

# Free Spirit's
# Laugh & Learn® Series

Solid information, a kid-centric point of view, and a sense of humor combine to make each book in our Laugh & Learn series an invaluable tool for getting through life's rough spots. For ages 8–13. *Paperback; 80–136 pp.; illust.; 5⅛" x 7"*

**www.freespirit.com**